NUTRI

NINJA®

Auto-iQ®

75 Nutritious & Delicious RECIPES

Nutritional Analyses: Calculations for the nutritional analyses in this book are based on the largest number of servings listed within the recipes. Calculations are rounded up to the nearest gram or milligram, as appropriate. If two options for an ingredient are listed, the first one is used. Not included are optional ingredients or serving suggestions.

Editors and Content: Katie Barry, Lauren Nelson, Karen Bedard

Recipe Development: SharkNinja® Culinary Innovation Team and Great Flavors Recipe Development Team

Graphic Designer: Leslie Anne Feagley

Creative/Photo Director: Keith Manning

Photography: Quentin Bacon and Gary Sloan

Published in the United States of America by

SharkNinja
89 A Street
Needham, MA 02494

AUTO-IQ, NINJA, NUTRI NINJA, and PRO EXTRACTOR BLADES are registered trademarks of SharkNinja Operating LLC.

BL480D ISBN: 978-1-4951-5245-0

10   9   8

Printed in China

Table of Contents

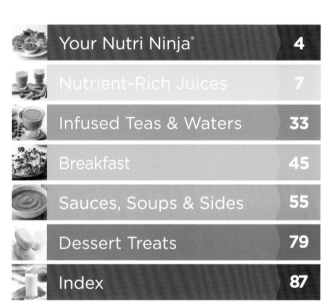

Your Nutri Ninja®	4
Nutrient-Rich Juices	7
Infused Teas & Waters	33
Breakfast	45
Sauces, Soups & Sides	55
Dessert Treats	79
Index	87

Follow us online for additional recipes and tips.

Your Nutri Ninja® with Auto-iQ®

Congratulations on starting your journey with your Nutri Ninja®.

Now you can easily blend whole fruits and vegetables into delicious juices, sauces, soups, dips, and desserts.

Ninja's powerful motor, intuitive Auto-iQ® Technology and a patented blade system can even handle hard ingredients, such as ice, kale, fibrous greens, pulpy fruits, flaxseed, and nuts.

Unique blending, pulsing, and pausing cycles deliver consistent results every time. No guesswork, just goodness.

New to this? We've got you covered. Choose from our delicious recipes. Plus, we have helpful tips to customize your own.

Check out ninjakitchen.com/recipes for additional recipes and tips.

Sweet Spinach Detox, page 20

The Nutri Ninja® with Auto-iQ® has three unique Nutri Ninja® Cups. We have provided some recommendations for each one.

SMALL
18-OUNCE

- Nutrient Extractions
- Smoothies
- Frozen Treats
- Protein Shakes
- Sauces & Dips
- Dressings

REGULAR
24-OUNCE

- Nutrient Extractions
- Smoothies
- Frozen Treats
- Protein Shakes
- Sauces & Dips
- Soups

JUMBO MULTI-
SERVE 32-OUNCE

- Nutrient Extractions
- Smoothies
- Frozen Dessert Drinks
- Soups

⚠ **CAUTION:** Remove the Pro Extractor Blades® Assembly from the Nutri Ninja® Cup upon completion of blending. Do not store ingredients before or after blending them in the cup with the blade assembly attached. Some foods may contain active ingredients or release gases that will expand if left in a sealed container, resulting in excessive pressure buildup that can pose a risk of injury. For ingredient storage in the cup, use only Spout Lid to cover.

Why Nutrient & Vitamin Extraction?*

Nutrient juices provide you with a simple way to boost your daily recommended nutritional intake. Key benefits include:

- Slower absorption of nutrients vs. juicing—more continual energy source
- Good source of nutrition—easy way to get your daily servings of fruits and vegetables
- Great variety of ingredients, textures, and flavor options
- Can be a quick and easy meal replacement
- Easy additions of protein and "good fats"
- Unlike juicing, adds fiber to your diet

Extract a drink containing vitamins and nutrients from fruits and vegetables.

Power Ball, page 16

Island Mood Boost,
page 28

7

PREP TIME: 5 minutes   SERVINGS: 2   CONTAINER: Regular 24-ounce Nutri Ninja® Cup

Watermelon Cooler

Ingredients

¼ ripe pear, seeded, cut in half

2 large fresh basil leaves

2 cups fresh watermelon chunks, chilled

Directions

1 Place all ingredients into the Regular 24-ounce Nutri Ninja® Cup in the order listed.

2 Select Auto-iQ® ULTRA BLEND.

3 Remove blades after blending.

PREP TIME: 5 minutes   SERVINGS: 4   CONTAINER: Jumbo Multi-Serve 32-ounce Nutri Ninja® Cup

Sangrita

Ingredients

1 small celery stalk, cut into 1-inch pieces

½ small lime, peeled and seeded

½ small orange, peeled and seeded

⅛ small white onion

2 small vine-ripened tomatoes, seeded and cut into quarters

½ cup carrot juice

2 dashes hot sauce or to taste

Pinch celery seed

1½ cups ice

Celery stalks and orange wedges for garnish, optional

Directions

1 Place all ingredients into the Jumbo Multi-Serve 32-ounce Nutri Ninja® Cup in the order listed.

2 Select Auto-iQ® ULTRA BLEND.

3 Remove blades after blending.

PREP TIME: 5 minutes   SERVINGS: 1   CONTAINER: Regular 24-ounce Nutri Ninja® Cup

Mango Melon Mint Fusion

Ingredients

½ cup honeydew melon chunks

½ cup fresh mango chunks

½ cup cantaloupe chunks

3 mint leaves

½ cup water

¾ cup ice

Directions

1 Place all ingredients into the Regular 24-ounce Nutri Ninja® Cup in the order listed.

2 Select Auto-iQ® BLEND.

3 Remove blades after blending.

TRY BASIL INSTEAD OF MINT FOR A DIFFERENT VARIATION.

Spicy Pineapple Recharge

Ingredients

½ jalapeño pepper, seeded

½-inch piece peeled fresh ginger

1 lime, peeled and cut in half

2 cups fresh pineapple chunks

⅔ cup orange juice

½ cup ice

Directions

1 Place all ingredients into the Regular 24-ounce Nutri Ninja® Cup in the order listed.

2 Select Auto-iQ® ULTRA BLEND.

3 Remove blades after blending.

Cool Honeydew Cleanser

Ingredients

2-inch piece peeled
cucumber, cut in half

½ cup fresh honeydew
melon chunks

½ cup fresh pineapple
chunks

¼ cup water

¼ cup ice

Directions

1 Place all ingredients into the
Small 18-ounce Nutri Ninja® Cup
in the order listed.

2 Select Auto-iQ® ULTRA BLEND.

3 Remove blades after blending.

Total Garden Drink

Ingredients

2 baby carrots

6-inch piece of cucumber, cut into 2-inch chunks

2-inch piece celery stalk

10 green grapes

¼ vine-ripened tomato, cut in half

4 hulled fresh strawberries

¼ small raw beet, peeled

1 cup fresh watermelon chunks

2 tablespoons cashews

1 tablespoon flax seeds

½ cup ice

Directions

1 Place all ingredients into the Jumbo Multi-Serve 32-ounce Nutri Ninja® Cup in the order listed.

2 Select Auto-iQ® ULTRA BLEND.

3 Remove blades after blending.

Tropical Chill

Ingredients

1 small ripe banana

½ cup fresh pineapple chunks

½ cup fresh honeydew melon chunks

¼ lime, peeled

¾ cup coconut water

1 cup ice

Directions

1 Place all ingredients into the Regular 24-ounce Nutri Ninja® Cup in the order listed.

2 Select Auto-iQ® ULTRA BLEND.

3 Remove blades after blending.

NINJA KNOW-HOW **ADD 1 TO 2 TEASPOONS FLAXSEED FOR A FIBER BOOST**

Lean Green Ninja

Ingredients

½ small ripe banana

¼ cup packed baby spinach

¼ cup packed kale leaves

¼ cup fresh pineapple chunks

¼ cup fresh mango chunks

¼ cup coconut water

¼ cup ice

Directions

1 Place all ingredients into the Small 18-ounce Nutri Ninja® Cup in the order listed.

2 Select Auto-iQ® BLEND.

3 Remove blades after blending.

PREP TIME: 5 minutes   SERVINGS: 1   CONTAINER: Small 18-ounce Nutri Ninja® Cup

Power Ball

Ingredients

½ small ripe banana

1 cup unsweetened light coconut milk

1 teaspoon unsweetened cocoa powder

1 cup frozen blueberries

Directions

1 Place all ingredients into the Small 18-ounce Nutri Ninja® Cup in the order listed.

2 Select Auto-iQ® ULTRA BLEND.

3 Remove blades after blending.

Frozen Kale Cacao

Ingredients

½ cup packed kale leaves

1 small frozen banana, cut into quarters

2 pitted dates

1 teaspoon unsweetened cocoa powder

1 scoop chocolate protein powder

1¼ cups unsweetened coconut milk

¼ cup ice

Directions

1 Place all ingredients into the Small 18-ounce Nutri Ninja® Cup in the order listed.

2 Select Auto-iQ® ULTRA BLEND.

3 Remove blades after blending.

PREP TIME: **5 minutes**   SERVINGS: 1   CONTAINER: Small 18-ounce Nutri Ninja® Cup

Pineapple Pleaser

Ingredients

½ cup fresh mango chunks

2 teaspoons almond butter

¾ cup original rice milk

¾ cup frozen pineapple chunks

Directions

1 Place all ingredients into the Small 18-ounce Nutri Ninja® Cup in the order listed.

2 Select Auto-iQ® ULTRA BLEND.

3 Remove blades after blending.

SUBSTITUTE RICE MILK WITH COW'S MILK OR ALMOND MILK IF PREFERRED.

PREP TIME: 5 minutes   SERVINGS: 2   CONTAINER: Jumbo Multi-Serve 32-ounce Nutri Ninja® Cup

Antioxidant Refresher

Ingredients

¼ cup coarsely chopped red cabbage

1 celery stalk, cut into quarters

¾ green apple, unpeeled, cut into quarters

¾ cup fresh blueberries

½ cup fresh watermelon chunks

¾ cup ice

Directions

1 Place all ingredients into the Jumbo Multi-Serve 32-ounce Nutri Ninja® Cup in the order listed.

2 Select Auto-iQ® ULTRA BLEND.

3 Remove blades after blending.

PREP TIME: 5 minutes   SERVINGS: 1   CONTAINER: Small 18-ounce Nutri Ninja® Cup

Sweet Spinach Detox

Ingredients

⅓ cup packed baby spinach

¼-inch piece peeled fresh ginger

¾ green apple, unpeeled, cut into thirds

¼ lemon, peeled and seeded

2 teaspoons agave nectar or honey

⅛ cup apple juice

⅛ cup water

¼ cup ice

Directions

1 Place all ingredients into the Small 18-ounce Nutri Ninja® Cup in the order listed.

2 Select Auto-iQ® ULTRA BLEND.

3 Remove blades after blending.

PREP TIME: 5 minutes   SERVINGS: 1   CONTAINER: Small 18-ounce Nutri Ninja® Cup

You're Making Me Bananas

Ingredients

½ orange, peeled and cut in half

¾ cup sweetened almond milk

¼ teaspoon ground nutmeg

1 small frozen banana, cut in half

Directions

1 Place all ingredients into the Small 18-ounce Nutri Ninja® Cup in the order listed.

2 Select Auto-iQ® ULTRA BLEND.

3 Remove blades after blending.

ADD KALE OR SPINACH TO SNEAK SOME GREENS INTO YOUR DIET.

Spiced Cucumber

Ingredients

6-inch piece cucumber, cut into 1-inch chunks

1 cup fresh cantaloupe chunks

½ jalapeño, seeded

¾ cup green seedless grapes

1¼ cups water

¾ cup ice

Directions

1 Place all ingredients into the Jumbo Multi-Serve 32-ounce Nutri Ninja® Cup in the order listed.

2 Select Auto-iQ® ULTRA BLEND.

3 Remove blades after blending.

Ninja 9

Ingredients

4-inch piece celery stalk

½ small green apple, cut into 4 quarters

4-inch piece carrot, peeled

⅛ small red onion

¼ jalapeño pepper, seeded

¼ small raw beet, peeled

¼ cup roughly chopped red cabbage

1½ vine-ripened tomatoes, cut into quarters

4-inch piece peeled cucumber, cut into quarters

¼ teaspoon sea salt

½ cup ice

Directions

1 Place all ingredients into the Jumbo Multi-Serve 32-ounce Nutri Ninja® Cup in the order listed.

2 Select Auto-iQ® ULTRA BLEND.

3 Remove blades after blending.

Ginger Pear Defense

Ingredients

1 ripe pear, cored, cut into quarters

½ cup fresh cantaloupe chunks

¼ lemon, peeled and seeded

½-inch piece peeled fresh ginger

½ cup ice

Directions

1 Place all ingredients into the Small 18-ounce Nutri Ninja® Cup in the order listed.

2 Select Auto-iQ® BLEND.

3 Remove blades after blending.

PREP TIME: 5 minutes   SERVINGS: 1   CONTAINER: Small 18-ounce Nutri Ninja® Cup

Berries Galore

Ingredients

½ cup fresh blackberries

¼ cup fresh raspberries

¼ cup fresh blueberries

1 orange, peeled and cut into quarters

¼ cup ice

Directions

1 Place all ingredients into the Small 18-ounce Nutri Ninja® Cup in the order listed.

2 Select Auto-iQ® ULTRA BLEND.

3 Remove blades after blending.

PREP TIME: **5 minutes**   SERVINGS: **1**   CONTAINER: **Small 18-ounce Nutri Ninja® Cup**

Strawberry Banana Smoothie

Ingredients

½ small ripe banana

½ cup low-fat milk

2 teaspoons agave nectar

½ cup frozen strawberries

Directions

1 Place all ingredients into the Small 18-ounce Nutri Ninja® Cup in the order listed.

2 Select Auto-iQ® ULTRA BLEND.

3 Remove blades after blending.

Pear Cleanse

Ingredients

1 cup packed baby spinach

½ cup fresh cilantro leaves

1¼ ripe pear, cored, cut into quarters

¼ ripe avocado, pitted and peeled

1 teaspoon fresh lime juice

1 pitted date

½ cup water

½ cup ice

Directions

1 Place all ingredients into the Jumbo Multi-Serve 32-ounce Nutri Ninja® Cup in the order listed.

2 Select Auto-iQ® ULTRA BLEND.

3 Remove blades after blending.

PREP TIME: **5 minutes**   SERVINGS: 1   CONTAINER: Small 18-ounce Nutri Ninja® Cup

Island Mood Boost

Ingredients

½ cup fresh pineapple chunks

½ small ripe banana

1 cup coconut water

½ cup frozen strawberries

½ cup frozen mango chunks

Directions

1 Place all ingredients into the Small 18-ounce Nutri Ninja® Cup in the order listed.

2 Select Auto-iQ® ULTRA BLEND.

3 Remove blades after blending.

Green Detox Splash

Ingredients

¾ Golden Delicious apple, unpeeled, uncored, cut into eighths

¾ cup loosely packed kale leaves

⅓ cup loosely packed parsley leaves

1½ teaspoons fresh lemon juice

½ small ripe banana

½ cup water

½ cup ice

Directions

1 Place all ingredients into the Jumbo Multi-Serve 32-ounce Nutri Ninja® Cup in the order listed.

2 Select Auto-iQ® ULTRA BLEND.

3 Remove blades after blending.

PREP TIME: 5 minutes   SERVINGS: 1   CONTAINER: Small 18-ounce Nutri Ninja® Cup

Berry Healthy Smoothie

Ingredients

½ cup packed baby spinach

¼ cup hulled fresh strawberries

¼ cup fresh blueberries

½ cup fresh mango chunks

¼ cup fresh pineapple chunks

¼ cup water

¼ cup ice

Directions

1 Place all ingredients into the Small 18-ounce Nutri Ninja® Cup in the order listed.

2 Select Auto-iQ® ULTRA BLEND.

3 Remove blades after blending.

DO NOT BLEND HOT INGREDIENTS.

Ginger Greens

Ingredients

¾ cup packed baby kale leaves

¼ cup loosely packed fresh cilantro leaves

¼ ripe avocado, pitted and peeled

1 pitted date

2 ripe kiwis, peeled and quartered

1 teaspoon fresh lime juice

¼-inch piece peeled fresh ginger

¼ cup coconut water

¼ cup ice

Directions

1 Place all ingredients into the Small 18-ounce Nutri Ninja® Cup in the order listed.

2 Select Auto-iQ® ULTRA BLEND.

3 Remove blades after blending.

PREP TIME: 5 minutes   SERVINGS: 1   CONTAINER: Regular 24-ounce Nutri Ninja® Cup

Butternut Squash Blast

Ingredients

¾ cup cooked, cooled butternut squash

¾ cup unsweetened vanilla almond milk

⅛ cup walnut pieces

1½ teaspoons real maple syrup

1 teaspoon ground turmeric

½ teaspoon ground cinnamon

½ cup ice

Directions

1 Place all ingredients into the Regular 24-ounce Nutri Ninja® Cup in the order listed.

2 Select Auto-iQ® BLEND.

3 Remove blades after blending.

DO NOT BLEND HOT INGREDIENTS.

Almond Chai Tea,
page 43

PREP TIME: 5 minutes   SERVINGS: 2   CONTAINER: Regular 24-ounce Nutri Ninja® Cup

Tropical Fruit Tea

Ingredients

½ cup fresh ripe papaya chunks

3 dried figs, stemmed and cut in half

1½ cups strongly brewed, chilled
mango passion fruit tea

1 cup frozen pineapple chunks

Directions

1 Place all ingredients into the Regular
24-ounce Nutri Ninja® Cup in the order listed.

2 Select Auto-iQ® BLEND.

3 Remove blades after blending.

DO NOT BLEND HOT INGREDIENTS.

NINJA KNOW-HOW   **YOU CAN USE PITTED DATES IN PLACE OF THE DRIED FIGS.**

Apple, Spice 'n' Everything Nice

Ingredients

¼ cup golden raisins

½ red apple, seeded and cut in half

2 packets (.035 ounces each) stevia

1½ cups strongly brewed, chilled apple tea

1 cup ice

Directions

1 Place all ingredients into the Regular 24-ounce Nutri Ninja® Cup in the order listed.

2 Select Auto-iQ® BLEND.

3 Remove blades after blending.

DO NOT BLEND HOT INGREDIENTS.

PREP TIME: 5 minutes   SERVINGS: 2   CONTAINER: Regular 24-ounce Nutri Ninja® Cup

Cherry Dragon Tea

Ingredients

1½ cups strongly brewed, chilled cherry tea

2 tablespoons honey

1¼ cups frozen dark sweet cherries

Directions

1 Place all ingredients into the Regular 24-ounce Nutri Ninja® Cup in the order listed.

2 Select Auto-iQ® BLEND.

3 Remove blades after blending.

DO NOT BLEND HOT INGREDIENTS.

Green Tea Detox Tonic

Ingredients

1¼ cups red leaf lettuce

2-inch piece cucumber, cut in half

2 packets (.035 ounces each) stevia

2¼ cups strongly brewed, chilled green tea

1¼ cups frozen mixed berries

Directions

1 Place all ingredients into the Jumbo Multi-Serve 32-ounce Nutri Ninja® Cup in the order listed.

2 Select Auto-iQ® ULTRA BLEND.

3 Remove blades after blending.

DO NOT BLEND HOT INGREDIENTS.

PREP TIME: 5 minutes   SERVINGS: 2   CONTAINER: Jumbo Multi-Serve 32-ounce Nutri Ninja® Cup

Cherry Limeade

Ingredients

1½ cups frozen cherries

3 tablespoons fresh lime juice

3 cups coconut water

Directions

1 Place all ingredients into the Jumbo Multi-Serve 32-ounce Nutri Ninja® Cup in the order listed.

2 Select Auto-iQ® BLEND.

3 Pour mixture through a fine-mesh strainer to extract the flavored water.

4 Remove blades after blending.

5 Store in refrigerator for up to 3 days.

Coconut Mango Energyade

Ingredients

¼ cup ripe mango chunks

1½ cups coconut water

6 fresh mint leaves

Directions

1 Place all ingredients into the Small 18-ounce Nutri Ninja® Cup in the order listed.

2 Select Auto-iQ® BLEND.

3 Remove blades after blending.

4 Store in refrigerator for up to 3 days.

Grape Apple Water

Ingredients

1 cup green grapes

½ green apple, seeded and cut in half

1½ cups cold water

Sweetener to taste

Directions

1 Place all ingredients into the Regular 24-ounce Nutri Ninja® Cup in the order listed.

2 Select Auto-iQ® ULTRA BLEND.

3 Pour mixture through a fine-mesh strainer to extract the flavored water.

4 Remove blades after blending.

5 Store in refrigerator for up to 3 days.

 TRY A TOUCH OF HONEY AS A NATURAL SWEETENER IN THIS DRINK.

PREP TIME: 4 minutes   SERVINGS: 4   CONTAINER: Jumbo Multi-Serve 32-ounce Nutri Ninja® Cup

Ginger Peach Lemonade

Ingredients

2¾ cups lemonade

1⅔ cups frozen peach slices

½-inch piece peeled fresh ginger

Sweetener to taste

Directions

1 Place all ingredients into the Jumbo Multi-Serve 32-ounce Nutri Ninja® Cup in the order listed.

2 Select Auto-iQ® BLEND.

3 Remove blades after blending.

4 Store in refrigerator for up to 3 days.

NINJA KNOW-HOW TRY A TOUCH OF HONEY AS A NATURAL SWEETENER IN THIS DRINK.

Pineapple Mint Water

Ingredients

½ cup fresh pineapple chunks

6 fresh mint leaves

3 cups cold water

Sweetener to taste

Directions

1 Place all ingredients into the Jumbo Multi-Serve 32-ounce Nutri Ninja® Cup in the order listed.

2 Select Auto-iQ® BLEND.

3 Pour mixture through a fine-mesh strainer to extract the flavored water.

4 Remove blades after blending.

5 Store in refrigerator for up to 3 days.

NINJA KNOW-HOW — TRY A TOUCH OF AGAVE NECTAR AS A NATURAL SWEETENER IN THIS DRINK.

Almond Chai Tea

Ingredients

3 pitted dates

2 tablespoons raw almonds

¼ small ripe banana

1¼ cups chilled, strongly brewed chai tea

Directions

1 Place all ingredients into the Small 18-ounce Nutri Ninja® Cup in the order listed.

2 Select Auto-iQ® ULTRA BLEND.

3 Remove blades after blending.

DO NOT BLEND HOT INGREDIENTS.

PREP TIME: 5 minutes   SERVINGS: 2   CONTAINER: Regular 24-ounce Nutri Ninja® Cup

Strawberry Basil Water

Ingredients

1 cup hulled fresh strawberries

¼ cup packed fresh basil leaves

2 cups cold water

Sweetener to taste

Directions

1 Place all ingredients into the Regular 24-ounce Nutri Ninja® Cup in the order listed.

2 Select Auto-iQ® BLEND.

3 Remove blades after blending.

4 Pour mixture through a fine-mesh strainer to extract the flavored water.

5 Store in refrigerator for up to 3 days.

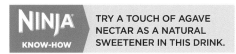

NINJA KNOW-HOW — TRY A TOUCH OF AGAVE NECTAR AS A NATURAL SWEETENER IN THIS DRINK.

Spinach & Feta Strata,
page 53

PREP TIME: 5 minutes   SERVINGS: 1   CONTAINER: Small 18-ounce Nutri Ninja® Cup

Top O' the Mornin' Smoothie

Ingredients

1 small ripe banana, cut into quarters

½ teaspoon ground cinnamon

1 scoop vanilla protein powder

1 cup unsweetened vanilla almond milk

1 orange, peeled and cut into quarters

½ cup ice

Directions

1 Place all ingredients into the Small 18-ounce Nutri Ninja® Cup in the order listed.

2 Select Auto-iQ® BLEND.

3 Remove blades after blending.

Strawberry Protein Power

Ingredients

½ cup nonfat vanilla Greek yogurt

2 tablespoons honey

1 tablespoon fresh lime juice

1¼ cups unsweetened almond milk

1 scoop vanilla protein powder

1 cup frozen strawberries

Directions

1 Place all ingredients into the Small 18-ounce Nutri Ninja® Cup in the order listed.

2 Select Auto-iQ® BLEND.

3 Remove blades after blending.

PREP TIME: 5 minutes   SERVINGS: 1   CONTAINER: Small 18-ounce Nutri Ninja® Cup

Almond Wake Me Up

Ingredients

½ small ripe banana, cut in half

¾ cup unsweetened vanilla almond milk

2 tablespoons almond butter

⅛ teaspoon ground cinnamon

2 teaspoons pure maple syrup

½ cup ice

Directions

1 Place all ingredients into the Small 18-ounce Nutri Ninja® Cup in the order listed.

2 Select Auto-iQ® ULTRA BLEND.

3 Remove blades after blending.

PREP TIME: 7 minutes   SERVINGS: 1   CONTAINER: Small 18-ounce Nutri Ninja® Cup

Banana & Oats

Ingredients

1 small ripe banana

1 tablespoon walnut pieces

1 cup nonfat milk

½ cup cold, cooked oatmeal

¼ teaspoon ground cinnamon

½ cup nonfat vanilla yogurt

Directions

1 Place all ingredients into the Small 18-ounce Nutri Ninja® Cup in the order listed.

2 Select Auto-iQ® BLEND.

3 Remove blades after blending.

PREP TIME: 5 minutes   SERVINGS: 1   CONTAINER: Small 18-ounce Nutri Ninja® Cup

Bright Side Mocha Shake

Ingredients

½ small ripe banana

¼ cup chilled coffee

1½ tablespoons almond butter

1 teaspoon unsweetened cocoa powder

1 teaspoon agave nectar

½ cup unsweetened almond milk

Dash sea salt

1 cup ice

Directions

1 Place all ingredients into the Small 18-ounce Nutri Ninja® Cup in the order listed.

2 Select Auto-iQ® BLEND.

3 Remove blades after blending.

DO NOT BLEND HOT INGREDIENTS.

Banana Sweet Potato Blast

Ingredients

4 pitted dates

¾ cup cooked, cooled sweet potato

1 small ripe banana, cut in half

¼ teaspoon ground nutmeg

1 cup nonfat milk

1 cup ice

Directions

1 Soak the dates in 1 cup warm water for 30 minutes. Drain; set aside.

2 Place the dates and remaining ingredients into the Regular 24-ounce Nutri Ninja® Cup in the order listed.

3 Select Auto-iQ® BLEND.

4 Remove blades after blending.

PREP TIME: 5 minutes   COOK TIME: 5 minutes   MAKES: 4 servings
CONTAINER: Jumbo Multi-Serve 32-ounce Nutri Ninja® Cup

Buckwheat Boost Pancakes

Ingredients

1 cup buttermilk

1 large egg

3 tablespoons canola oil

½ cup buckwheat flour

½ cup all-purpose flour

1 teaspoon baking soda

1 teaspoon sugar

½ teaspoon salt

1 tablespoon honey

Directions

1 Place the buttermilk, egg, and canola oil into the Jumbo Multi-Serve 32-ounce Nutri Ninja® Cup.

2 Select START and blend for 5 seconds. Add the rest of the ingredients, except the honey, and blend for an additional 5 seconds. Add the honey and blend for 5 more seconds. Remove cup from the base and **remove the blade from the cup**. Cover the cup with plastic wrap and let sit for 1 hour.

3 Place a lightly oiled griddle or skillet over medium heat. Pour pancake batter in desired size and cook until small bubbles form. Flip and continue cooking until center is puffed and springs back when gently pushed.

DO NOT BLEND HOT INGREDIENTS.

PREP TIME: 5 minutes + 4 hours rest   COOK TIME: 25 minutes   MAKES: 8 servings
CONTAINER: Jumbo Multi-Serve 32-ounce Nutri Ninja® Cup

Spinach & Feta Strata

Ingredients

5 large eggs

1 cup half & half

½ cup Monterey Jack cheese, cubed

½ cup feta cheese, cubed

¼ teaspoon ground nutmeg

½ teaspoon salt

¼ teaspoon black pepper

1 cup cooked spinach, well drained (about 6 cups fresh)

1 loaf day-old French bread, crusts removed, torn into bite-sized pieces

Directions

1 Coat a round 9-inch baking pan with vegetable cooking spray. Place the torn bread into the pan; set aside.

2 Place the eggs, half & half, Monterey Jack cheese, feta cheese, nutmeg, salt, and pepper to the Jumbo Multi-Serve 32-ounce Nutri Ninja® Cup.

3 PULSE 5 times, using short pulses. Add the spinach and PULSE 2 more times, until incorporated.

4 Remove blades after blending.

5 Pour the spinach and egg mixture over the bread. Place into the fridge for 4 hours to allow the egg mixture to soak into the bread.

6 Preheat oven to 350°F. Bake 20 to 25 minutes, until puffed and golden brown. Serve warm.

DO NOT BLEND HOT INGREDIENTS.

PREP TIME: 10 minutes   MAKES: 2 servings   CONTAINER: Regular 24-ounce Nutri Ninja® Cup

Tomato Basil Scramble

Ingredients

4 large eggs

¼ cup vine-ripe tomato, deseeded

¼ cup mozzarella

¼ cup loosely packed fresh basil leaves

⅛ teaspoon salt

⅛ teaspoon ground black pepper

Directions

1 Place all ingredients into the Regular 24-ounce Nutri Ninja® Cup in the order listed. PULSE until finely chopped.

2 Coat a non-stick sauté pan with cooking spray and place over medium-high heat. Cook the eggs, stirring frequently, until fluffy and cooked through.

3 Remove blades after blending.

NINJA KNOW-HOW   SUBSTITUTE 6 LARGE EGG WHITES FOR A LOWER-CHOLESTEROL BREAKFAST.

*Curried Carrot Soup,
page 68*

PREP TIME: 5 minutes   MAKES: 1 ¼ cups   CONTAINER: Regular 24-ounce Nutri Ninja® Cup

Classic Hummus

Ingredients

1 can (14 ounces) garbanzo beans, drained and liquid reserved

¼ cup plus 2 tablespoons garbanzo bean liquid

2 tablespoons fresh lemon juice

2 tablespoons olive oil

1 clove garlic

1 tablespoon tahini

½ teaspoon ground cumin

½ teaspoon salt

Directions

1 Place all ingredients into the Regular 24-ounce Nutri Ninja® Cup in the order listed.

2 Select Auto-iQ® ULTRA BLEND.

3 Remove blades after blending.

Salsa Verde

Ingredients

¼ small yellow onion, cut in half

¼ jalapeño, seeded

1 garlic clove, peeled

3 tablespoons flat-leaf parsley

⅓ cup packed fresh cilantro

½ poblano or Anaheim pepper, seeded and cut in chunks

4 tomatillos, peeled and cut in quarters

¼ cup extra-virgin olive oil

1 tablespoon fresh lime juice

¼ teaspoon kosher salt

Directions

1 Place all ingredients into the Regular 24-ounce Nutri Ninja® Cup in the order listed.

2 Select START and blend for 15 to 20 seconds.

3 Remove blades after blending.

PREP TIME: 10 minutes   MAKES: 2 ½ cups   CONTAINER: Regular 24-ounce Nutri Ninja® Cup

Smokey Sweet Pepper Dip with Crostini

Ingredients

2-inch piece French bread, cut in half

2 tablespoon olive oil

1 can (14 ounces) garbanzo beans, drained

1 jar (4 ounces) roasted red peppers, drained

1 clove garlic

1 tablespoon balsamic vinegar

½ teaspoon smoked paprika

½ teaspoon salt

¼ teaspoon black pepper

Directions

1 Preheat oven broiler to high. Lightly brush bread slices with oil on one side and place under the broiler pan, oiled side up. Broil until toasted; set aside to cool slightly.

2 Place the toasted bread and remaining ingredients into the Regular 24-ounce Nutri Ninja® Cup. Select START and blend until smooth. Taste and adjust seasonings. Serve alongside pita chips and fresh vegetables.

3 Remove blades after blending.

DO NOT BLEND HOT INGREDIENTS.

PREP TIME: 10 minutes   MAKES: 1 cup   CONTAINER: Small 18-ounce Nutri Ninja® Cup

Pineapple Cilantro Dipping Sauce

Ingredients

1 cup fresh pineapple chunks

½ jalapeño pepper, seeded

¼ small white onion, cut in half

¼ cup fresh cilantro leaves

1½ tablespoons fresh lime juice

1 tablespoon coconut oil

salt and pepper to taste

Directions

1 Place all ingredients into the Small 18-ounce Nutri Ninja® Cup in the order listed.

2 Select START and blend for 15 seconds.

3 Remove blades after blending.

 KNOW-HOW STORE CILANTRO IN A WET PAPER TOWEL IN THE CRISPER DRAWER TO KEEP FRESH.

PREP TIME: 10 minutes MAKES: 6 servings CONTAINER: Small 18-ounce Nutri Ninja® Cup

Tabbouleh Dip

Ingredients

3-inch piece cucumber, cut into quarters

¼ small yellow onion, cut in half

2 tablespoons fresh mint leaves

½ cup loosely packed parsley leaves

1½ vine-ripe tomatoes, cut into quarters

¼ teaspoon ground black pepper

¼ teaspoon salt

1 tablespoon olive oil

1 tablespoon fresh lemon juice

Directions

1 Place all ingredients into the Small 18-ounce Nutri Ninja® Cup in the order listed.

2 Select START and blend for 15 seconds.

3 Remove blades after blending.

 NINJA® KNOW-HOW SERVE THIS AS AN ACCOMPANIMENT TO GRILLED FISH, BEEF, OR LAMB.

PREP TIME: 25 minutes   COOK TIME: 9 minutes   MAKES: 10 servings   CONTAINER: Small 18-ounce Nutri Ninja® Cup

French Onion Dip

Ingredients

1 tablespoon vegetable oil

1 medium yellow onion, chopped

½ teaspoon salt

¼ teaspoon ground black pepper

3 tablespoons malt vinegar

6 ounces nonfat cream cheese, softened

½ cup nonfat sour cream

Directions

1 In a 10-inch sauté pan at medium heat, add the oil, onion, salt and black pepper. Cook for 6 to 8 minutes or until caramelized, stirring occasionally. Add the malt vinegar and cook for 1 minute.

2 Remove from the heat and let cool for 10 minutes.

3 Place the cooked onion mixture, tofu, cream cheese and sour cream into the Small 18-ounce Nutri Ninja® Cup.

4 Select START and blend for 15 seconds.

5 Remove blades after blending.

DO NOT BLEND HOT INGREDIENTS.

PREP TIME: 10 minutes   COOK TIME: 25 minutes   MAKES: 1 ¾ cups
CONTAINER: Small 18-ounce Nutri Ninja® Cup

Fresh & Healthy Ketchup Relish

Ingredients

¾ cup yellow onion, peeled, cut in quarters, divided

½ red bell pepper, seeded, chopped

1 clove garlic

2 vine-ripe tomatoes, seeded and cut in quarters

1 tablespoon plus 2 teaspoons apple cider vinegar

½ teaspoon molasses

¼ teaspoon ground black pepper

¾ cup kosher baby dill pickles, cut in half

1 tablespoon Dijon mustard

Directions

1 Place the ½ small yellow onion, red bell pepper, garlic, tomatoes, apple cider vinegar, molasses and ground black pepper into the Small 18-ounce Nutri Ninja® Cup.

2 Select Auto-iQ® BLEND.

4 Remove blades after blending.

5 Pour the tomato mixture into a 2-quart saucepot and cook on medium heat for 25 minutes, stirring occasionally.

6 Remove from the heat and pour into an airtight container and refrigerate for 1 hour.

7 Place the ¼ small yellow onion, pickles, Dijon mustard and the cooled tomato mixture into the Small 18-ounce Nutri Ninja® Cup.

8 PULSE 6 times or to desired consistency is achieved.

DO NOT BLEND HOT INGREDIENTS.

PREP TIME: 25 minutes   COOK TIME: 30 seconds   MAKES: 1 ½ cups   CONTAINER: Regular 24-ounce Nutri Ninja® Cup

Kale & Sunflower Pesto

Ingredients

¼ medium bunch kale, stems removed

¼ cup loosely packed fresh basil leaves

1 small garlic clove

2 tablespoons unsalted, roasted sunflower seeds

2 tablespoons parmesan cheese

Zest and juice of ½ lemon

¼ cup water

Sea salt to taste

Fresh ground pepper

¼ cup olive oil, plus more as needed

Directions

1 Bring 4 quarts of salted water to a boil. Blanch the kale leaves for 30 seconds and upon removal, immediately plunge into ice water. Squeeze the kale leaves dry and set aside.

2 Add the kale, basil, garlic, sunflower seeds, Parmesan cheese, lemon juice/zest, olive oil, and a pinch of salt and pepper to the Regular 24-ounce Nutri Ninja® Cup.

3 PULSE 5 times and then BLEND continuously until desired pesto consistency is achieved. Add more oil if needed. Set aside.

4 Remove blades after blending.

DO NOT BLEND HOT INGREDIENTS.

PREP TIME: 5 minutes   COOK TIME: 25 minutes   MAKES: 2–4 servings   CONTAINER: Regular 24-ounce Nutri Ninja® Cup

Sun-Dried Tomato Sauce

Ingredients

½ onion, peeled and cut in quarters

½ tablespoon canola oil

2 cloves garlic

1 can (14 ounces) whole peeled tomatoes and juice

3 ounces sun-dried tomatoes packed in olive oil

¼ cup dry red wine

¼ teaspoon red pepper flakes

⅛ bunch basil, chopped

Salt and pepper to taste

Directions

1 Place all ingredients into the 24-ounce Nutri Ninja® Cup in the order listed. Select START and blend until smooth.

2 Place sauce into a medium saucepan and bring to a boil over medium heat. Reduce heat and simmer 20 to 25 minutes.

3 Remove blades after blending.

Best Blender Salsa

Ingredients

1 can (14 ounces) whole peeled tomatoes

½ white onion, peeled and quartered

½ jalapeno, seeds removed

½ chipotle chili, in adobo

1 tablespoon adobo sauce

½ lime, peeled and quartered

salt and pepper to taste

Directions

1 Place all ingredients into the Regular 24-ounce Nutri Ninja® Cup in the order listed.

2 PULSE until desired consistency is achieved.

3 Remove blades after blending.

 FOR A TROPICAL TWIST, ADD ½ CUP FRESH MANGO TO CUP BEFORE PULSING.

PREP TIME: 15 minutes   COOK TIME: 30 minutes   MAKES: 4 servings   CONTAINER: Jumbo Multi-Serve 32-ounce Nutri Ninja® Cup

Cream of Sweet Potato Soup

Ingredients

1 tablespoon olive oil

½ medium yellow onion, chopped

½ teaspoon salt

¼ teaspoon ground black pepper

2¾ cups sweet potatoes, cut into
1-inch chunks

2 cups unsalted vegetable broth

¾ cup light cream

Directions

1 Preheat a 3-quart saucepot on medium-low heat. Add the oil and onions and sauté, stirring occasionally, until translucent, 3 to 5 minutes.

2 Add the salt, black pepper, sweet potatoes and vegetable broth. Bring to a boil, reduce the heat to medium-low, and cook 20 to 25 minutes or until the sweet potatoes are fork-tender.

3 Remove from heat and cool to room temperature.

4 Place the cooled sweet potato mixture into the Jumbo Multi-Serve 32-ounce Nutri Ninja® Cup.

5 Select Auto-iQ® BLEND.

6 Remove blades after blending.

7 Place the pureed sweet potato mix back into saucepan stir in the light cream; simmer until heated through.

DO NOT BLEND HOT INGREDIENTS.

White Bean & Cabbage Soup

Ingredients

2 teaspoons olive oil

1 clove garlic

1 small yellow onion, chopped

1 celery stalk, chopped

⅓ cup chopped green pepper

2 cups chopped green cabbage

½ teaspoon salt

¼ teaspoon ground black pepper

⅛ teaspoon dried oregano leaves

3 cups unsalted vegetable broth

1 can (15 ounces) cannellini beans, drained and rinsed

Directions

1 Place a 3-quart saucepan over medium-low heat. Add the oil, garlic, onions, celery and green pepper. Cook for 7 minutes.

2 Add the green cabbage, salt, black pepper, oregano, and vegetable broth. Bring to a boil, reduce the heat to medium-low and cook 30 to 35 minutes.

3 Remove from heat and cool to room temperature.

4 Working in two batches, place half of the cooled soup into the Jumbo Multi-Serve 32-ounce Nutri Ninja® Cup.

5 Select Auto-iQ® BLEND.

6 Remove blades after blending.

7 Place the pureed soup into a medium bowl and continue with remaining soup. Return all pureed soup back to the saucepan and add the cannellini beans; simmer until heated through.

DO NOT BLEND HOT INGREDIENTS.

Curried Carrot Soup

Ingredients

2 teaspoons olive oil

3 cloves garlic

¾ medium yellow onion, cut into 3 pieces

¼ teaspoon salt

¼ teaspoon ground black pepper

2 teaspoons red curry paste

2¼ cups carrots, peeled and cut into 1-inch chunks

2¼ cups low-sodium chicken broth

1¼ cups light coconut milk

Directions

1 Place a 3-quart saucepan over medium heat. Add the oil and sauté the garlic and onions 3 to 5 minutes, stirring until translucent.

2 Add the salt, black pepper, red curry paste, carrots, and chicken broth to the saucepan. Bring to a boil, reduce heat to medium-low, and cook 20 to 25 minutes or until the carrots are fork-tender.

3 Remove from heat, add the coconut milk, and cool to room temperature.

4 Working in two batches, place half of the cooled soup into the Jumbo Multi-Serve 32-ounce Nutri Ninja® Cup.

5 Select Auto-iQ® BLEND.

6 Remove blades after blending.

7 Place the pureed soup into a medium bowl and continue with remaining soup. Return all pureed soup back to the saucepan and simmer until heated through.

DO NOT BLEND HOT INGREDIENTS.

PREP TIME: 10 minutes   MAKES: 4 servings   CONTAINER: Jumbo Multi-Serve 32-ounce Nutri Ninja® Cup

Cucumber Avocado Soup

Ingredients

1½ avocados, pitted, peeled, and cut into quarters

⅓ yellow pepper, seeded and cut in half

½ jalapeño, seeded and cut in half

⅓ cup packed cilantro leaves

1 clove garlic

½ teaspoon salt

1 tablespoon fresh lemon juice

1½ cups low-sodium chicken broth

6-inch piece cucumber, cut into 1-inch chunks

Directions

1 Place all ingredients into the Jumbo Multi-Serve 32-ounce Nutri Ninja® Cup in the order listed.

2 Select Auto-iQ® BLEND.

3 Remove blades after blending.

4 Chill before serving.

PREP TIME: 15 minutes   COOK TIME: 15 minutes   MAKES: 2 servings   CONTAINER: Regular 24-ounce Nutri Ninja® Cup

Chilled Spanish Tomato Soup

Ingredients

2-inch piece of baguette, quartered

1 cup warm water

3 vine-ripe tomatoes, cored and quartered

1 clove garlic

⅛ cup dry roasted almonds

¼ cup olive oil

¾ teaspoon sherry vinegar

¾ teaspoon salt

⅛ teaspoon ground black pepper

Directions

1 Place the baguette and warm water into a small bowl and let sit for 10 minutes, allowing the bread to soften. In a mesh strainer set over a medium bowl, squeeze out the tomato seeds from each quartered piece. Set the quartered, cleaned tomatoes aside. Push the seeds around in the mesh strainer to release as much liquid as possible. Reserve the extracted liquid and discard the remaining seeds.

2 Squeeze the baguette of excess liquid and place baguette into the Regular 24-ounce Nutri Ninja® Cup. Add the tomatoes, tomato liquid, garlic, almonds, olive oil, sherry vinegar, salt, and pepper.

3 PULSE 3 times, using short pulses, then select START and blend for 45 seconds.

4 Remove blades after blending.

5 Chill at least 2 hours before serving. Adjust seasonings and garnish with your desired toppings!

DO NOT BLEND HOT INGREDIENTS.

 NINJA KNOW-HOW — WE RECOMMEND TOPPING THIS SILKY SMOOTH SOUP WITH CHOPPED HARD BOILED EGGS AND FRESH CUT CHIVES.

PREP TIME: 15 minutes   COOK TIME: 35 minutes   MAKES: 4 servings   CONTAINER: Jumbo Multi-Serve 32-ounce Nutri Ninja® Cup

Kale & Celery Root Soup

Ingredients

2 teaspoons olive oil

2 garlic cloves, peeled and chopped

¾ small yellow onion, chopped

½ bulb celery root, peeled and chopped

2 cups packed kale leaves, chopped

1 teaspoon salt

½ teaspoon ground black pepper

3 cups unsalted vegetable broth

Directions

1 Preheat a 5-quart saucepan over medium heat. Add the oil, garlic, and onions. Gently stir to sauté 3 to 5 minutes or until translucent.

2 Add the remaining ingredients, bring to a boil, reduce heat to medium-low and simmer 20 to 25 minutes or until the celery root is fork-tender.

3 Remove from heat and cool to room temperature.

4 Working in two batches, place half of the cooled soup into the Jumbo Multi-Serve 32-ounce Nutri Ninja® Cup.

5 Select Auto-iQ® BLEND. Return pureed soup to saucepan and simmer until heated through.

6 Remove blades after blending.

DO NOT BLEND HOT INGREDIENTS.

PREP TIME: 10 minutes   MAKES: 1 cup   CONTAINER: Small 18-ounce Nutri Ninja® Cup

Basil Mayonnaise

Ingredients

¾ cup packed fresh basil leaves

¾ cup light mayonnaise

1 teaspoon Dijon mustard

1 teaspoon fresh lime juice

½ teaspoon salt

2 teaspoons cold water

Directions

1 Place all ingredients into the Small 18-ounce Nutri Ninja® Cup in the order listed.

2 PULSE until desired consistency is achieved, using long pulses.

3 Remove blades after blending.

NINJA KNOW-HOW SERVE ATOP TURKEY BURGERS, CHICKEN PANINI, OR EVEN FISH.

PREP TIME: 10 minutes   MAKES: 1 ¾ cups   CONTAINER: Regular 24-ounce Nutri Ninja® Cup

Apricot-Mustard Dressing

Ingredients

½ cup apricot jam

2 tablespoons Dijon mustard

¼ cup rice wine vinegar

3 tablespoons honey

2 tablespoons fresh thyme, stems removed

½ teaspoon salt

3 tablespoons olive oil

¾ cup nonfat sour cream

Directions

1 Place all ingredients into the Regular 24-ounce Nutri Ninja® Cup in the order listed.

2 PULSE 3 times, using short pulses, then select START and blend for 45 seconds.

3 Remove blades after blending.

NINJA KNOW-HOW — YOU CAN SUBSTITUTE GRADE B MAPLE SYRUP FOR THE HONEY.

PREP TIME: 5 minutes   MAKES: 12 ounces   CONTAINER: Small 18-ounce Nutri Ninja® Cup

Carrot Ginger Dressing

Ingredients

1 large carrot, peeled and cut into chunks

1 shallot, peeled and halved

2-inch piece peeled fresh ginger

1 tablespoon tamari or soy sauce

2 tablespoons rice wine vinegar

1 tablespoon roasted sesame seed oil

¼ cup grape seed oil or other neutral vegetable oil

2 tablespoons water

Directions

1 Place all ingredients into the Small 18-ounce Nutri Ninja® Cup in the order listed.

2 Select START and blend for 30 seconds, or until desired consistency is achieved.

3 Remove blades after blending.

PREP TIME: 15 minutes   MAKES: 1 ¼ cups   CONTAINER: Small 18-ounce Nutri Ninja® Cup

Everyday Vinaigrette

Ingredients

½ cup packed fresh cilantro, stems removed

⅓ cup packed flat-leaf parsley, stems removed

2 tablespoons roughly chopped chives

1 clove garlic

¼ teaspoon ground black pepper

¼ teaspoon salt

1 tablespoon Dijon mustard

¼ cup apple cider vinegar

¾ cup olive oil

Directions

1 Place all ingredients into the Small 18-ounce Nutri Ninja® Cup in the order listed.

2 Select START, and blend for 25 seconds, or until desired consistency is achieved.

3 Remove blades after blending.

PREP TIME: 10 minutes   MAKES: 2 cups   CONTAINER: Regular 24-ounce Nutri Ninja® Cup

Avocado Caesar Dressing

Ingredients

1 ripe avocado, pitted and cut in half

3 cloves garlic

1-inch chunk (1½ ounces) Parmesan cheese

2 oil-cured anchovy filets

½ teaspoon ground black pepper

2 tablespoons fresh lemon juice

2 tablespoons apple cider vinegar

1 cup cold water

⅛ teaspoon salt

Directions

1 Place all ingredients into the Regular 24-ounce Nutri Ninja® Cup in the order listed.

2 Select START, and blend for 30 seconds, or until desired consistency is achieved.

3 Remove blades after blending.

NINJA KNOW-HOW SERVE DRESSING WITH A ROMAINE SALAD; FOR A FULL MEAL, ADD GRILLED CHICKEN BREAST OR SALMON.

PREP TIME: 15 minutes   MAKES: 1 cup   CONTAINER: Small 18-ounce Nutri Ninja® Cup

Supreme Goddess Dressing

Ingredients

3 tablespoons rice wine vinegar

2 tablespoons Dijon mustard

2 tablespoons light mayonnaise

¼ cup low-fat sour cream

¼ cup olive oil

1 clove garlic

¼ teaspoon salt

⅛ teaspoon ground black pepper

¼ cup loosely packed fresh parsley leaves

2 tablespoons loosely packed fresh tarragon leaves

2 tablespoons fresh dill sprigs

1 scallion, cut into 4 pieces

Directions

1 Place all ingredients into the Small 18-ounce Nutri Ninja® Cup in the order listed.

2 Select START, and blend for 20 seconds, or until desired consistency is achieved.

3 Remove blades after blending.

PREP TIME: 5 minutes   MAKES: 2 cups   CONTAINER: Regular 24-ounce Nutri Ninja® Cup

Asian Marinade

Ingredients

⅓ cup rice wine vinegar

½ cup low-sodium soy sauce

½ lime, peeled

½ lemon, peeled and seeded

½ orange, peeled and seeded

1 tablespoon ground coriander

½-inch piece peeled fresh ginger

3 cloves garlic

2 scallions, each cut in half

Directions

1 Place all ingredients into the Regular 24-ounce Nutri Ninja® Cup in the order listed.

2 Select START, and blend for 30 seconds, or until desired consistency is achieved.

3 Remove blades after blending.

Tropical Fresh Fruit
Ice Pops,
page 86

Dessert Treats

PREP TIME: 5 minutes   MAKES: 4 servings   CONTAINER: Regular 24-ounce Nutri Ninja® Cup

Hawaiian Frappe

Ingredients

½ small ripe banana

1 cup frozen pineapple chunks

1 cup coconut water

1 tablespoon coconut oil

1 cup ice

Directions

1 Place all ingredients into the Regular 24-ounce Nutri Ninja® Cup in the order listed.

2 Select START and blend for 30 seconds.

3 Remove blades after blending.

PREP TIME: 5 minutes   MAKES: 2 servings   CONTAINER: Regular 24-ounce Nutri Ninja® Cup

Frozen Chocolate Treat

Ingredients

1 cup low-fat milk, separated

¼ cup instant nonfat dry milk

2½ tablespoons unsweetened cocoa powder

2 tablespoons agave nectar

Pinch salt

1½ cups ice

Directions

1 In a bowl, combine ½ cup of the milk with the instant nonfat dry milk, cocoa powder, agave, and salt. Stir with a whisk or a fork until all ingredients have formed a smooth slurry.

2 Add the ice to the Regular 24-ounce Nutri Ninja® Cup followed by the slurry and the last ½ cup of milk.

3 Select Auto-iQ® ULTRA BLEND.

4 Remove blades after blending.

PREP TIME: 5 minutes   MAKES: 4 servings   CONTAINER: Regular 24-ounce Nutri Ninja® Cup

Banana Chocolate Mousse

Ingredients

2 small ripe bananas, peeled and cut into quarters

2 ripe avocados, pitted, peeled, and cut into quarters

¼ cup chocolate syrup

Juice of half an orange

¼ cup unsweetened cocoa powder

Directions

1 Place all ingredients into the Regular 24-ounce Nutri Ninja® Cup in the order listed.

2 PULSE 3 times, using short pulses, then select START and blend for 45 seconds.

3 Remove blades after blending.

 NINJA KNOW-HOW MICROWAVE 2 OUNCES OF DARK CHOCOLATE INSTEAD OF SYRUP FOR A RICHER FLAVOR.

Monkey Madness

Ingredients

1½ small ripe bananas

2 tablespoons plus 1 teaspoon unsweetened cocoa powder

1½ cups sweetened almond milk

2 tablespoons agave nectar

⅓ cup almond butter

1½ cups ice

Directions

1 Place all ingredients into the Jumbo Multi-Serve 32-ounce Nutri Ninja® Cup in the order listed.

2 Select START and blend for 30 seconds.

3 Remove blades after blending.

Cherry Cheesecake Dip

Ingredients

¾ cup dried cherries

1 tablespoon unsweetened almond milk

1 tablespoon almond butter

1 packet (.035 ounce) stevia

1 package (8 ounces) nonfat cream cheese, softened

1⅓ cups frozen dark sweet cherries, thawed

Directions

1 Place all ingredients into the Regular 24-ounce Nutri Ninja® Cup in the order listed.

2 PULSE for 10 times, then select START and blend for 15 seconds.

3 Remove blades after blending.

PREP TIME: 5 minutes   MAKES: 4 servings   CONTAINER: Jumbo Multi-Serve 32-ounce Nutri Ninja® Cup

Vanilla Nut Frozen Treat

Ingredients

⅔ cup vanilla oat milk

½ cup walnut pieces

¼ teaspoon pure vanilla extract

1 packet (.035 ounce) stevia

¾ cup nonfat vanilla Greek yogurt

2½ cups ice

Directions

1 Place all ingredients into the Jumbo Multi-Serve 32-ounce Nutri Ninja® Cup in the order listed.

2 Select Auto-iQ® ULTRA BLEND.

3 Remove blades after blending.

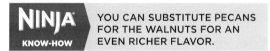

NINJA KNOW-HOW

YOU CAN SUBSTITUTE PECANS FOR THE WALNUTS FOR AN EVEN RICHER FLAVOR.

PREP TIME: 5 minutes   MAKES: 8 popsicles
CONTAINER: Jumbo Multi-Serve 32-ounce Nutri Ninja® Cup

Tropical Fresh Fruit Ice Pops

Ingredients

1¼ cups fresh mango chunks

2¾ cups fresh pineapple chunks

2 tablespoons agave nectar

Directions

1 Place all ingredients into the Jumbo Multi-Serve 32-ounce Nutri Ninja® Cup in the order listed.

2 Select Auto-iQ® BLEND.

3 Remove blades after blending.

4 Pour into popsicle molds and freeze overnight or until solid.

Index

NUTRIENT-RICH EXTRACTIONS
Antioxidant Refresher, **19**
Berries Galore, **25**
Berry Healthy Smoothie, **30**
Butternut Squash Blast, **32**
Cool Honeydew Cleanser, **12**
Frozen Kale Cacao, **17**
Ginger Greens, **31**
Ginger Pear Defense, **24**
Green Detox Splash, **29**
Island Mood Boost, **28**
Lean Green Ninja, **15**
Mango Melon Mint Fusion, **10**
Ninja 9, **23**
Pear Cleanse, **18**
Pineapple Pleaser, **18**
Power Ball, **16**
Sangrita, **9**
Spiced Cucumber, **22**
Spicy Pineapple Recharge, **11**
Strawberry Banana Smoothie, **26**
Sweet Spinach Detox, **20**
Total Garden Drink, **13**
Tropical Chill, **14**
Watermelon Cooler, **8**
You're Making Me Bananas, **21**

INFUSED TEAS & WATERS
Almond Chai Tea, **43**
Apple, Spice 'n Everything Nice, **35**
Cherry Dragon Tea, **36**
Cherry Limeade, **38**
Coconut Mango Energyade, **39**
Ginger Peach Lemonade, **41**
Grape Apple Water, **40**
Green Tea Detox Tonic, **37**
Pineapple Mint Water, **42**
Strawberry Basil Water, **46**
Tropical Fruit Tea, **34**

BREAKFAST
Almond Wake Me Up, **48**
Banana & Oats, **49**
Banana-Sweet Potato Blast, **51**
Bright Side Mocha Shake, **50**
Buckwheat Boost Pancakes, **52**
Spinach & Feta Strata, **53**
Strawberry Protein Power, **47**
Tomato Basil Scramble, **54**
Top O' the Mornin' Smoothie, **46**

SAUCES, SOUPS & SIDES
Asian Marinade, **78**
Apricot-Mustard Dressing, **73**
Avocado Caesar Dressing, **76**
Basil Mayonnaise, **72**

Best Blender Salsa, **65**
Carrot Ginger Dressing, **74**
Chilled Spanish Tomato Soup, **70**
Classic Hummus, **56**
Cream of Sweet Potato Soup, **66**
Cucumber Avocado Soup, **69**
Curried Carrot Soup, **68**
Everyday Vinaigrette, **75**
French Onion Dip, **61**
Fresh & Healthy Ketchup Relish, **62**
Kale & Celery Root Soup, **71**
Kale & Sunflower Pesto, **63**
Pineapple Cilantro Dipping Sauce, **59**
Salsa Verde, **57**
Smokey Sweet Pepper Dip with Crostini, **58**
Sun-Dried Tomato Sauce, **64**
Supreme Goddess Dressing, **77**
Tabbouleh Dip, **60**
White Bean & Cabbage Soup, **67**

DESSERT TREATS
Banana Chocolate Mousse, **82**
Cherry Cheesecake Dip, **84**
Frozen Chocolate Treat, **81**
Hawaiian Frappe, **80**
Monkey Madness, **83**
Tropical Fresh Fruit Ice Pops, **86**
Vanilla Nut Frozen Treat, **85**

NUTRI NINJA® Auto-iQ®

75 Nutritious & Delicious RECIPES